"What do I hate most about celebrity chefs? The way they put on some weird affectation to sell their books!"

Striped Galah
2020

For Hugo, Jess and Angus

1st Edition, 2020

Produced and Printed by Waving Man Productions

Reviews of *The Cash-Poor & Hungover University Students' Cook-book*

"Once in a generation a cook-book comes along, written by an outsider, a maverick, which takes cuisine by the scruff of the neck and becomes the new standard. I keenly await that book"

Cucina Oggi

"About as interesting as your stupid calendar Striped!"

Vladimir Putin

"A cook-book targeting a readership with no money? Interesting business proposition Striped!"

John Maynard Keynes

"The graduating body voted Striped most likely to be caught in a compromising position with a goat and bottle of tomato sauce. Striped has always had a thing for food."

Sampson Peruvic

"I knew Striped when he was just a Boroko night-club chanteuse, jongleur and Petomane Artist. He was as breath-taking then as his cooking is now."

Ernest Hemingway

Also by the Same Author

Calendario alla Putinesca (with collected thoughts), 2017

Coming soon....

Striped's follow-up Christmas cook-book:

"Blood on the Feztive Bird"

Acknowledgements

Many thanks indeed to Liz Coughlan who over many hours took and processed all of the great photographs for this book. If any of the photos are poorly framed, badly lit, have light reflection or are a little fuzzy, they were mine!

Many thanks also to contributors, especially Paul "Chimpy" Chamberlin, Emma Macdonald and Tanya Landwehr, who not only shared recipes but significantly improved my personal recipe armoury.

And finally a big thanks to my wonderful wife Clare, for not rolling her eyes too much while I undertake these projects.

Contents

Forward

Going to university is exciting for a whole bunch of reasons, which I won't bore you with here; you already know them. But for many of you, for the first time in your life, two utterly tragic conditions will collide.

Firstly, you will be "poor". Every purchase you make will be measured in the number of beers you could have bought if you didn't buy that thing. And no student should be without beer!

Secondly, you will be on your own when it comes to food. Your parents won't be there to fill the cupboards and make you a decent feed. You might eat at the uni canteen or college cafeteria, but it won't be great and the cost will be high (meaning less beer!).

For many students, this means a terrible diet of tasteless food. Others will live on fast food. This book will avoid such a calamity!

These recipes have been collected because they are perfect for students, meaning:

1. They are dead easy. Restaurant chefs can make a perfect meal, exactly the same, every time. Cooks make good food that is different every time. You will be a cook. If you don't have one of the ingredients or you do something a bit different to the directions, it won't matter, the food will still be good. This is why there are few measures for the ingredients – just get some and chuck it in!
2. Most are really quick. When you're studying for exams you have no spare time but you have to eat – just try studying when you're hungry! But you don't have to resort to corn flakes or cuppa-noodles (both of which are great by the way). Besides, 30-60 minutes is perfect brain-break to get you back into the study feeling fresher.

3. Those that aren't quick, will feed you for at least two days. Or let you feed friends who are invited to eat, as long as they bring the beer (notice the trend yet?). Besides, left-overs are a wonderful thing; just re-heat (if you can be bothered) and scoff it down. In many recipes I've shown different things you can do with the left-overs.
4. They are all flexible. You can leave out, put in or substitute all sorts of ingredients so there is no need to stress too much about what you have or haven't got. You can also experiment, so these meals shouldn't get old and tired in a hurry. In each recipe I've shown alternative and additional ingredients that you can use.
5. They will be fun. Because you can't go wrong, there is no stress. Which means you can put on some music and enjoy a drink or two.

There are a couple of recipes in here that break these rules just a little. They might be a little more expensive or a bit more involved to make. But they are never both. I've included them because sometimes you might want to take it up a notch.

Even if cooking never becomes a passion for you, it should be fun. There are few things I enjoy more than cooking a great dish, with my wife Clare managing the sounds, keeping me company and of course keeping my glass full. Cooking is best with lubrication!

Enjoy!

What Your Cupboard MUST have in it.

Listed below are some things that you really shouldn't be without. They are the key ingredients for many of the recipes in this book. You can also do almost anything with them. So just get them.

Carbs

These guys are the fillers that will make sure your meal fills you up and goes a long way. Some of them are pretty tasty in their own right too.

- Spaghetti or any other pasta.
- Potatoes (don't buy soft or green ones)
- Decent bread. Rule of thumb, if its sliced when you buy it, it might be OK but you can find better. None of that white rubbish! Good bread is a revelation.
- Rice. Brown if you can get it.

Fats

You can't do without fats for cooking.

- Olive oil. Get extra virgin if you can afford it. Olive oil is the most versatile and best oil for cooking (but get a different oil if want to stir fry) and just about the only oil for adding to a salad (yes you will learn a few salads too).
- Salted butter. Much tastier than margarine.

Tinned Food

This stuff can sit in your cupboard forever, but it won't because they are great for simple cooking.

- Canned chopped tomatoes (try to keep about 4).
- Canned tuna (in olive oil is better than in water/brine).
- Baked beans.

Other Stuff (some of the World's great foods)

- Eggs
- Vegemite (tough luck if you don't live in Australia or the UK)
- Garlic
- Lemons
- Salt (sea-salt if you can afford it as it tastes better)
- Cayenne pepper (let's spice it up a little)

What Your Kitchen <u>MUST</u> have in it.

When you leave home and go to uni, you almost certainly can't rely on your parents to buy you the right kitchen gear. And you certainly can't expect to get it right first time yourself.

Either way you will need this list.

If you are an artist or a tradesperson, you will know that good tools make all the difference. Good kitchen gear can make all the difference between cooking being fun and successful versus a pain in the arse and a failure. So buy the best you can and look after your tools!

- Knives are the work-horse of the kitchen. Make sure that you have a minimum of three. One with about a 12 inch blade (2.54 cm to the inch – work it out yourself) for the heavy lifting. One with 4-6 inch blade for "delicate" stuff. And a bread knife. This last one is critical because you won't have the time or inclination to keep your knives sharp. It will be essential for cutting tomatoes and meat, as well as bread.
- A potato peeler. You will peel all sorts of vegetables with it and life in the kitchen without one is so much harder (use the small knife mentioned above if you don't have a peeler).
- A potato masher. You won't use it too often but if you don't have one you will miss it.
- A grater with small holes (I don't know how else to describe this). You will zest (grate the rind off) lemons and other citrus fruit a lot and it is next to impossible to do without one of these. "But I can just use the juice" I hear you say. "Bullshit" I respond. The zest has loads more flavour. You will also use it for cheese. Whether you like it or not you will also sometimes use it to grate off knuckle skin and I can tell you THAT is no fun and a grater with small holes does less damage.

- A plastic egg flip. Eggs are a student's dream: easy, cheap, packed with protein and fat and bursting with addictive flavour. A plastic flip won't scratch the surface of your frying pan.
- A wooden spoon (for a non-scratch stirrer).
- At least two pots, preferably three. One for the big meals (stews, soups, etc), a medium one for cooking pasta amongst other things, and a small one if you are doing small stuff (like heating up a can of baked beans). Try to get heavy pots as they keep their heat a lot better and are less likely to blacken when you heat food too fast. Also try to get pots with non-plastic handles so you can put them in the oven with the lid on. Glass lids are great as you don't have to take the lid off to see if the food is boiling.
- A good frying pan, preferably also with a glass lid and a non-plastic handle that will cope with being put under a griller.
- A colander, for draining pasta and potatoes (spuds).
- Willing fingers. A lot of ingredients need mixing with some others and your hands are perfect for this and there are few foods that aren't nice to touch. So have a rummage! If you can, also keep your kitchen sink with some soapy water in it so you can clean them quickly and move on to the next step.

If someone gives you a microwave oven, sell it and buy some of the abovementioned stuff (or beer). Food takes time (not much, but some) for the ingredients to blend while cooking and do their magic. If you don't believe me, take almost any of the recipes in this cook-book, chuck them in a pot, heat it up and as soon as it is hot have a taste. It likely will taste like the separate ingredients. Try it again in a little bit of time and the story is totally different. A microwave is also a totally functional tool with zero theatre and passion!

I know you have precious little time, which is one of the reasons for this book. But a microwave oven is a race to the bottom.

Some Cooking Rules of Thumb

This stuff is easy but important to know. They will quickly become ingrained in your memory and you will cook using these tricks without even thinking about it.

- **Spices**. If you are using cayenne pepper or any other spices, frying them in the oil for a minute or two before adding other ingredients will draw out the flavour and make the kitchen smell wonderful.
- **Salt**. It's better to cook with salt as it enhances the flavour. This works better than adding salt to the meal after you have put it on a plate, but if you forgot the salt or just want more, have at it. It is possible to overdo the salt, so add some, taste and add more until you get it to your likings.
- **Garlic and Onion**. These will need to be fried in oil before adding most other ingredients, to draw out the flavour and break them down a bit (un-fried onions can be tough to eat). Chuck them in with the spices if you like (see above). They are sufficiently fried when they have browned a little (golden brown). Try not to over fry garlic – if it goes dark brown it starts to get bitter.
- **Vegetables**. No matter how you cook them, they are best when still a little firm as they taste better, are more nutritious and feel better in your mouth. So when you're cooking them, take a small bite periodically and stop cooking when you're happy with them. If you are cooking different vegetables together, like when boiling or roasting in a single pan, try to cut the hardest vegetables (potatoes, carrots, etc) into smaller pieces than softer vegetables (pumpkin, zucchini, etc). This will help them to be ready at more or less the same time. If after checking them you find that one of the harder vegetables is taking longer than expected, just cut them into smaller pieces and put them back in the pan.
- **Minced Meat**. Whether using beef, pork or chicken mince, it will need to be browned by frying before adding any vegetables or liquid ingredients.

Stewed mince is not very nice. Best to chuck it in the pan when any spices and garlic/onion (see above) have been fried.

- **Carbs**. No matter what the recipe in this book, if it calls for pasta, bread, rice or spuds, they are fully replaceable and if you don't have the one you want, just use another.
- **Pasta and Rice**. When you cook these, stir frequently at the start so that they don't stick together. Use the cooking time in the instructions as a rule of thumb. There is no substitute for fishing some of it out of the pot and taking a bite. When properly cooked, they will not be hard but not be soft or stodgy either; they will have a little resistance to the bite. But more importantly just cook it until you think it tastes good and feels nice in your mouth. You can cook pasta and rice before the rest of the meal is ready, drain and cool it in cold water and then immerse it in hot or boiling water just before serving (this is a good way of de-stressing the meal as you don't need multiple parts ready all at the same time).

The Dead Simple Stuff

To be honest, you should have made these numerous times before you left home, but as they say, to assume makes an ass out of u and me.

These are probably the easiest, fastest and cheapest recipes in this book and you will make them often. So using the variations section of the recipes and mixing it up a bit will keep them fresh.

Roast (or Baked) Spuds

What is the difference between roasting and baking? Don't know and don't care!

This has to be about the cheapest meal you can make. It's also tasty, filling, flexible and dead easy. All you need is a potato, a pan for boiling water and an oven.

The best roast spuds have an outer skin that is quite hard, crispy and therefore tasty. I recommend pre-boiling the spud so the inside cooks quickly and then pop it in the oven to roast.

Essential Ingredients

Spuds (1 for each meal or person eating, it doesn't matter how big they are)

Butter

Optional Ingredients

Sweet Potatoes

Salt

Cheese (grated or thinly sliced)

Cayenne pepper

A can of baked beans

A can of tuna

A can of corn kernels

Directions

Turn your oven on to 200-220C or thereabouts.

Clean the spud but don't peel it. Chuck it in a pot of water and boil it until you can poke a fork in and it goes in reasonably easily towards the middle. This means it is close to cooked through.

Pull out the spud and chuck it in the oven, on aluminium foil or something that will catch any drips. This will finish the cooking and give it a crispy skin. Check the spud at about the 30 minute mark and see if the skin is how you want it. Just put it back in the oven for more if you want to.

Cut it up (enjoying the steam and aroma) and put loads of butter on it. Done! Cheese placed on top will melt over the spud nicely too.

Variations

You can put almost anything on the spud. Here are some suggestions.

When the spud is close to ready, heat up the other ingredients (except the cheese and spices) in a pot and pour it over the cut spud, putting the cheese and any spices on top.

- Baked beans
- Canned tuna
- Baked beans and tuna
- Canned corn and tuna
- Any left-overs from other meals. Any pasta sauce is great on a spud.
- Any of the dips from later in this book.

Also try sweet potatoes instead of normal spuds. Wonderful.

Left-Overs

You won't have any! Although, strictly speaking, you can cook multiple spuds and put them in the fridge and just chuck them in the oven to reheat.

Toasted Sandwiches

You WILL make these and you WILL like them! You just need a griller.

Essential Ingredients

Bread

Cheese

Optional Ingredients

Fresh Tomato (thinly sliced)

A can of baked beans

A can of tuna (in olive oil but drain off the oil)

A tin of corn (drain off the liquid)

A tin of sardines (drain off the liquid)

Sliced ham, salami or any other sliced meat

Left-overs

Cayenne pepper

Directions

Toast or grill your bread on both sides until it is the way you like it.

Slice your cheese and put it on the toast. Try to make sure that the entire surface of the toast is covered with cheese. Any uncovered areas will toast more and might burn. Cheese will probably overflow the toast so make sure you are toasting on or above some aluminium foil.

When the toast is melted, take it out and try to eat it without burning your mouth (good luck with that).

Variations

You can put almost anything on the toast. Here are some suggestions. There are only two things to consider: 1) cheese always goes on top; and 2) best to put the ingredient on thinly so it heats up under the melting cheese (unless you want to heat it up first!)

- Tomato slices
- Baked beans
- Tuna
- Corn
- Sardines
- Sliced ham, salami or any other sliced meat
- Left-overs
- Any combination of the above
- Any of the above with pepper and/or cayenne sprinkled on top of the cheese before grilling.

Left-Overs

Chuck it in the fridge and eat it later cold.

Crostini (or Bruschetta)

First a lesson in pronunciation (yeh right, coming from an Aussie!). I'm no snob and my Italian is truly terrible (ask Clare my wife). But too many times I have cringed when hearing people ask for "broo-shet-a". Its "broo-sket-ta". Almost everyone can pronounce "lasagne" properly, without a hard "g" and a "nya" on the end, so I have no idea why bruschetta is so widely mispronounced. Just pronounce the "k" and the "t" twice and all will be put to rights. There. Rant over (don't get me started on tagliatelle).

The difference between these and toasted sandwiches is that:

1. you use a decent, long loaf of bread (you can for toasted sandwiches too but more often then not you will likely use regulation bread) and you will slice it yourself; and
2. (almost) never melt cheese on top.

These are so varied and simple that I'm simply going to list some of my favourites. You will get the point, understand the flexibility and hopefully be courageous enough to try your own thing.

Essential Ingredients

Bread

Almost anything else

Directions

Toast or grill your bread on both sides until it is the way you like it and then try the following (each example being a crostini or bruschetta in its own right). Make three or four different ones and this is a great starter for a meal or snack with drinks. All of these can be made without the garlic if you like, but why would you? You could also add some pesto from a jar to any of these (well the Italian looking ones anyway).

- Peel a raw garlic clove and rub it over the toasted bread. Drizzle with olive oil and sprinkle with salt.
- Peel a raw garlic clove and rub it over the toasted bread. Do the same with a tomato (cherry tomatoes are a handy size for this). Sprinkle with salt.
- Peel a raw garlic clove and rub it over the toasted bread. Lay a couple of preserved fruits, such as sun-dried tomatoes or capsicum slices, onto the toasted bread straight from the jar. Sprinkle with salt.
- Peel a raw garlic clove and rub it over the toasted bread. Lay a couple of anchovy fillets on the bread and drizzle with olive oil.
- Lay a thin slice of tomato on the toasted bread, do the same with mozzarella and a fresh basil leaf. Repeat the sequence if you have room on the toasted bread. Classic!
- Thinly slice butter and lay the slices on the toasted bread (scraping butter off the block just doesn't give you enough). Spread with a generous amount of vegemite. OK. This one is not like the others. But it IS great and holds its own in this company.
- Using a fork, make a mash of butter, grated or thinly sliced garlic and some anchovies. Spread it on the toasted bread. Clare once told me off for making this. Not because of its obvious passion-killing qualities. But because I threw it together at the end of a large plate she had prepared with meats, cheeses and a variety of other Summer aperitivi and this pungent mash was the best of the lot.
- Lay a thick slice of taleggio cheese on the toasted bread and stick it back under the griller to melt. Top it with miele di castagno (chestnut honey). This is one of the easy but a bit pricey dishes I spoke about. Taleggio is easy enough to get outside of Italy nowadays and is a really superb cheese. Miele di castagno might be harder to get (try an Italian grocery) but has an

utterly unique flavour. Reality is, you could use almost any cheese and any honey and it would still be great!

Left-Overs

You won't have any!

Mashed Spuds and Fried Eggs

Mashed potato is good. Fried eggs are good. Together, they are spectacular.

Essential Ingredients

Eggs

Potatoes (1 or 2 per person, depending on their size)

Butter

Salt

Optional Ingredients

Strictly speaking you could add any of the optional ingredients from the Lager-Frenzy Fry-Up recipe, but this dish is filling on its own and the simplicity is wonderful.

Directions

The spuds take the longest to cook and you want your eggs with runny yolks, so get the spuds ready first.

Peel the spuds and cut them up into smallish pieces (make an "OK" sign with your forefinger and thumb – about that size). Put them in a pot of water with the water level well above the spuds and boil them. They will be ready when you can easily insert a fork into the spuds without the spuds breaking apart. Drain them, mash them in the pot you used to cook them in, add butter and salt, mash them again and put them aside with the lid on. They will stay hot for quite a while.

Don't sweat it if the spuds are little lumpy. It doesn't change the taste and you can easily just mash them some more.

Fry the eggs using the method described in the Lager-Frenzy Fry-Up recipe. Don't worry if there is a little uncooked white on top of the egg. You will see why when you serve it.

Spoon the mashed potato onto a plate. Put a couple of fried eggs on top. Cut up the eggs, letting the yolk run into the mashed potato and mix everything together.

That's it! Sounds weird. Try it and I guarantee you will want it again.

Variations

Why are you reading this? I've already said to keep it simple and just follow the recipe!

Although, if you must know, the mash in the photo for this recipe has cut-up, left over shish taouk and chicken shawarma in it. Man it was good!

Left-Overs

You won't have any. But if you do, put it in the fridge. Spread on buttered bread, cold mashed potato makes a great sandwich.

Lightning Fast Pasta

There are some other pasta recipes later in the book that take a little more time (see Quick Pasta and Downright Slow Pasta) and taste better as a result, but this is seriously quick (lazy?) and cheap. So it has to be here for intense study days or when you're almost out of cash.

Essential Ingredients

Any Pasta

Any jar of Pasta Sauce or Pesto

Optional Ingredients

If you are going to add anything other than the options below, you may as well start with fresh ingredients, which defeats the purpose. This is meant to be lighting fast.

Cheese

Cayenne Pepper

Directions

Bring some water in a pot to the boil. Add the pasta and boil it until cooked (see Rules of Thumb for how to cook pasta).

Drain the pasta and put it in a bowl. Add a spoon or two of the pasta sauce or pesto straight from the jar and mix it together. The hot pasta will heat up the sauce.

Fini!

Variations

Add some cheese and/or cayenne pepper when mixing in the pasta sauce or pesto.

Left-Overs

Why would there be any? Its probably just as fast to make the meal again than reheat it!

Paupers' Pizza

Pizza is great for a late night feed after a night out (or in). But there is no reason to pay shop prices to get it delivered an hour after you feel hungry.

Make this and you will question buying delivered pizza again.

I used to buy pizza bases, make a small mountain of various ingredients with a crater in the middle and drop an egg into it before sticking it in the oven. My Italian friends would have died. But if that is your thing then have at it!

Traditional pizza has far fewer ingredients and I admit to now preferring that approach. And if you don't find one pizza filling enough using that technique then maybe just make two?

Essential Ingredients

Flat bread

Jar of pizza sauce

Cheese (Mozzarella is definitely best as it melts and browns really nicely and tastes great, but any cheese will do)

Optional Ingredients

Cayenne pepper

Pepper

Herbs

Anything that either is thin enough to cook quickly or heat up under a layer of melted cheese. Try some of the following, just remember that the more you have on the base the harder it will be for it to get crispy towards the centre.

- Thinly sliced garlic
- Anchovies
- Pickled jalapeno peppers
- Sliced olives
- Salami
- Sun-dried or semi sun-dried tomatoes
- Pickled capsicums
- Sliced mushrooms
- Any left-overs from another meal
- Anything else that takes your fancy

Directions

Heat your oven to 180C (350F).

Put some aluminium foil down on the tray you will cook the food on in the oven.

Put the flat bread on the foil and spread some pizza sauce over it.

Put the main ingredients onto the flat bread. My personal favourite is anchovies, jalapenos, salami and sliced olives.

Cover the pizza with sliced or grated cheese, plenty of it.

If using it, sprinkle cayenne pepper over the cheese.

Stick it in the oven and within 10-15 minutes you have a pizza. Keep checking the edges of the pizza base and when it is crispy/hard, it should be ready to eat. Remember, the ingredients shouldn't need much cooking or simply heating through and the cheese needs to melt. But the base should be crispy so be a little patient.

Variations

Unlimited. Just make it up as you go along.

But a special mention goes out to **Pizza For Desert!** Put your flat bread in the oven and when it is close to done spread on Nutella, stick it back and pull it out when ready. Surprisingly good!

Left-Overs

There shouldn't be any. But cold pizza from the fridge is pretty good.

The Sexier Stuff

These recipes take a little more effort but are still simple, quick and cheap. After making these a few times you will easily remember the ingredients and how to make it without referring to this book, which is great for when you decide to drop by the store after a night out and haven't planned ahead. With any of these, if you can buy the key ingredient or two you will definitely be able to get the rest, making shopping very easy.

Frittata (OK, its just an Omelette)

A frittata has parmesan cheese in it, but you probably won't be able to afford it so you will make it without, or replace it with another cheese like cheddar.

Either way, it is no longer a frittata. It's an omelette. Either way, it doesn't matter. It's wonderful, flexible and is a great way of re-using left-overs.

Essential Ingredients

Eggs (as many as you like, 2-3 for each meal or person eating)

Salt

Optional Ingredients

Cheese (grated or cut into very small pieces)

Bacon (cut into very small pieces)

Tomato (cut into very small pieces)

Capsicum (cut into very small pieces)

Mushrooms (cut into very small pieces)

Cayenne pepper

Almost anything else that takes your fancy and isn't wet (the omelette needs to be firm when cooked)

Directions

Whisk the eggs in a bowl with the salt, using an egg whisk or a fork. Put your arm into it!

If you are adding cheese you will need to grate it. But if you don't have a grater just cut it into very small pieces and add it to the eggs.

Heat the oil in a frying pan and add the cayenne or any other spices that you might be using. Fry for about a minute.

Add the optional ingredients to the pan (except the cheese) and fry for a couple of minutes.

Distribute the ingredients more or less evenly around the pan and then gently pour in the eggs/cheese.

Cook until done.

If you are using a lot of eggs your omelette may be thick and it take a long time for the surface to cook. To avoid this (and possibly over-cooking the bottom), use a low heat towards the end or, better still, chuck the frying pan under the grill.

Variations

- You really can use any vegetable that can be cooked by frying to soften it before the eggs are added. Small pieces speed up the cooking process.
- Add peas that have already been boiled.
- Use any left-over vegetables from a previous meal.
- Use any left over meat or chicken from a previous meal.

- If have the inclination, you can make it look nice by placing thinly sliced fresh tomato on top before putting it under the grill.
- If you mix the eggs and ingredients continuously while they are cooking you get scrambled eggs. Great on toast.

Left-Overs

- Served cold from the fridge the next day. Frittata is often served cold in Italy so this isn't such a weird idea.
- Cut it to the size of any bread that you have and make an omelette sandwich. Yes you can add tomato sauce if you have too!

Lager-Frenzy Fry-Up

At the very least, a good fry-up is simple, easy and bloody fantastic. After a boozy night it is a thing of wonder. It can be as simple as eggs on toast with bacon, but it can also be a minor feast.

The only thing to make every effort to get right, are the eggs. Eggs with a runny yolk are terrific. With a hard yolk they are still good but lose flavour. Here I show you how to make great eggs every time.

Essential Ingredients

Eggs

Salt

Bacon

Bread

Butter

Optional Ingredients

Pepper and/or Cayenne pepper

Banana (no joke!)

A can of baked beans

A can of spaghetti

Tomatoes (large or small)

Garlic

Mushrooms

Sausages

Left-overs

Directions

Put your bacon in a frying pan with some oil and fry it until it is the way you like it. Don't fry it at too hot a temperature if you want to avoid oil and fat spitting everywhere when they start to express water (which they will).

While your bacon is frying, toast or grill your bread on both sides until it is the way you like it. Butter your toast.

Eggs always come last because they are quick to cook and you want to serve them as soon as they are ready. To take the stress out of it, start the eggs when the toast and bacon are done (toast and bacon can be kept hot on a plate in a low temperature oven if you like.)

What you want is for the egg white to be hard and the yolk soft and runny. The eggs help you do this by having a white that hardens at a lower temperature than the yolk. But you can still use a few tricks to get the best possible result.

Crack the eggs into a frying pan, medium heat. If you break a yolk you won't be able to have a runny yolk, so its up to you whether you eat it anyway or scoop it out and do another one.

Fry the eggs until the white is almost cooked through, with just a little runny white on top. You are almost there. There are a couple of ways you can get the white on top to be hard but keeping a runny yolk.

1. Tilt the pan so the oil and left-over bacon fat pools at one end and spoon it a few times over the egg yolk and any runny egg white.
2. Add a drizzle of water and put a lid or a plate on the pan to keep the steam in as the water boils. After about 20 seconds lift the lid/plate and the white should be hard. If not, put the lid back and check again until you are happy with them.

Serve the eggs on the buttered toast with a little salt on the eggs (no salt on the bacon, which is already loaded with salt) and get stuck in. Breaking the yolk will let it run into the toast – yum!

Variations

These are really simple and will turn your fry-up into an orgy of flavour (oo-er!). The only limit really is how many pots and pans you have. Just remember, eggs come last!

- Sprinkle pepper and/or cayenne pepper on your eggs at the same time as the salt.
- Banana. Yes you heard right – banana. Slow fried banana is a revelation with bacon. Slice the banana in half down its length and slowly fry it on both sides in the oil and fat from the bacon. You want it to be soft to touch with your egg flip and golden brown on both sides (not black!) Serve it on top of the bacon.

- Baked beans or canned spaghetti (an abomination to my Italian friends). Simply chuck these alone or together into a pot and heat it up. It can stay on a low heat while you cook the other stuff so adding them to the meal is stress-free.
- Large tomatoes. The half tomatoes you get with a Full-English breakfast are almost always rubbish. They take a long time to grill or fry so they are usually served under-cooked. But if done right they are fab. Cut them in half, put a little salt (and cayenne pepper if you like) on the flat side and fry them on both sides, starting with the flat side down. Frying is preferably done at a relatively low temperature but will take some time so start them first, along with the bacon.
- Small (cherry) tomatoes. Put some oil in a small pot and fry some sliced garlic until it is golden brown but not over-cooked. You can also add cayenne pepper with the garlic. Cut the cherry tomatoes in half and put them in the pot along with some salt. Stew them over a lowish heat with a lid on until they are about half liquid (the tomatoes will break down and express their juice). Try them if you like to see if they are ready to eat.
- Mushrooms. Sliced mushrooms can be easily fried in the oil and fat from the bacon. Keep your olive oil handy as they will soak it up and you might need to add more. If they start to express water its no problem as they will start to fry again once the water is boiled off. Another option is simply to cook the sliced mushrooms in the same pot as the cherry tomatoes.
- Sausages. Just fry them with the bacon. Don't prick them or else they will start to dry out as they are cooking.
- Black pudding. Made of pork blood, spices and other unmentionables, this sausage is not for everyone. It will need slicing before frying.
- Left-overs. Almost any left overs can be reheated by frying in the oil and fat from the bacon.

Left-Overs

If there are left-overs you aren't trying hard enough (or are too hung over for even a fry-up to work!)

Quick Pasta (Fish and Citrus Pasta)

I first made this from what I could find in the cupboards of Clare's (my now wife's) kitchen. Worked a treat and I've been making ever since!

Essential Ingredients

Pasta

Tinned tuna in olive oil (1 or 2)

Garlic

Tinned chopped tomatoes (1 or 2)

One Lemon

Salt

Optional Ingredients

Cayenne Pepper and/or pepper

Different oily fish (e.g. salmon or mackerel)

Lime or other citrus fruit

Directions

Wash the lemon and, without cutting it, grate the rind so you have a small pile of lemon zest.

Drain the oil from the canned fish into a pot, add the garlic and cook until the garlic is golden brown.

Add everything else to the pot (the zest, but not the lemon) and bring them to a low boil (simmering). They are already cooked so just need heating up. Simmering for a while lets the flavours merge.

Bring some water in a pot to the boil. Add the pasta and boil it until cooked (see Rules of Thumb for how to cook pasta).

When the pasta is cooked, drain and put on a plate. Add as much sauce as you like.

Variations

If you like this recipe, some variations can make sure you don't get bored with it.

- Add cayenne when you fry the garlic.
- Any oily fish could be used, like salmon or mackerel.
- Any citrus fruit could be used, particularly lime. You could use orange as well but it is more subtle.

Left-Overs

Reheat any pasta and sauce together in a pot with the lid on and at low heat to stop it sticking. You might have to add some water.

Cook more pasta if needed.

The sauce is also great on a roast spud or toast.

Stuffed Pasta Chimpy

I have had too many memorable meals with my great friend (of 40 years!) Chimpy to remember, despite or maybe because of the copious quantities of fine wine they are usually accompanied by.

One of the best was when Chimpy & Emma visited Melbourne and we went to a classy restaurant to celebrate their engagement. Of course it is not possible to visit Melbourne in Winter without going to the Melbourne Cricket Ground (the MCG or simply the "G", seriously one of the great sporting venues of the World) to watch some Aussie Rules Football, which we did before going out to dinner. We were on strict instructions from our partners on where and when to meet after the game so we could clean up before our night out. And time was of the essence.

Well a great game and too much beer conspired against us. I hate that! I vaguely recall Chimpy saying at the end of the game something like "I didn't come all this way to not run onto the field". So when the final whistle blew we fell over the fence and ran about a bit, amongst hundreds of other fans that looked surprisingly only a fraction of our age.

We finally got to the pick up point and our carefully planned denial about not running onto the field was belied by the grass stains on our knees. Sprung badly!

We did get to the restaurant in time for our reservation and the total collection of my memories of the evening comprises lots of laughing, a magnificent bottle of Brokenwood red brought by Chimpy and Emma, an entrée of four scallops that had been cookie-cuttered to be small but perfectly formed (I really would have preferred the entire, natural scallops complete with gonad; I just don't get so-called haute cuisine) and going for the first and only time in my entire life to a toilet that required no touching of any surface whatsoever from entry to exit (the doors didn't give a Star Trek "shoosh" as they opened and closed but you can't have everything.)

Anyway, Chimpy got sight of an early draft of this cookbook and offered this recipe which is an absolute cracker.

Essential Ingredients

Any packaged, stuffed pasta (ravioli, tortellini, tortelloni, anything with any filling you like) bought from the refrigerated section of your supermarket

Oil

Cayenne pepper

Cream (about 250 mL, just enough to coat the pasta)

A generous splash of soy sauce

Optional Ingredients

Garlic

Sliced mushrooms

Vegemite (YES!)

Directions

This recipe is super quick. The stuffed pasta is cooked by plunging into a pot of boiling water and let cook based on the instructions on the pack, usually about 4 – 8 minutes. But there is no substitute for plucking one of the pasta pieces out of the water and biting the corner to see if it is done to your liking. Don't worry about the filling as it will be pre-cooked and only needs to be hot.

The only thing to remember about timing is that when you drain the pasta it will start to stick together if you don't put it into the sauce within a reasonable period of time. But no need to panic!

Prepare the sauce first by frying the cayenne pepper in the oil in a frying pan or large pot for a little bit and then adding the cream and the soy sauce. It will come to simmer pretty quickly and after a few minutes is good to go. Simply add the drained pasta, gently stir it so the pasta pieces don't break open and when the pasta is covered in the sauce its good to go.

Variations

Here are some options and additions to keep this recipe fresh.

- Add garlic when you fry the cayenne.
- Sliced mushrooms added to the pan when you fry the cayenne is also very good.
- Replace the soy sauce with vegemite. Marmite also works, as would any salty, strong tasting sauce.

Left-Overs

Niente.

Downright Slow Pasta (Pasta Bollogn-Eayrs)

So why would you want to make a pasta that might take you an hour and half to prepare and cook?

Because it is so good and will make so much sauce you can feed your mates or be eating it yourself for days. You can freeze it and eat it months later too.

Essential Ingredients

Olive oil

Garlic (the more the better)

Onion

Carrot

Mince meat (about 250g but more or less depending on whether you are a big meat-eater or not)

6-8 large fresh tomatoes

Salt

Cheese (Parmesan is best but almost any will do)

Pasta

Optional Ingredients

You will note below that tinned tomatoes is not an option because, while it would be quicker, it won't taste anywhere near as good as using fresh tomatoes. The whole point of this dish is to spend more time, for better results (and left-overs.)

Cayenne pepper

Fennel seeds (add these – you won't regret it)

Different minces

Capsicum

Zucchini

Mushrooms

Broccoli

Frozen peas

Brown beer or stout (and sugar)

Any herbs (preferably fresh but dried will do)

Directions

Thinly slice the garlic and onions. Peel and cut the carrot into small pieces. Fry them all together in a large pot with plenty of oil until the garlic is golden brown. The onion should be quite soft by now too.

Add the mince and keep stirring around until it has browned. A wooden spoon is good for this but you could use anything.

You want the mince to have broken up into small clumps so feel free to be rough with it.

Chop up the tomatoes, discarding the hard end and the core if it is hard. Add the tomatoes to the pot, along with any tomato juice on your chopping board or plate.

Add salt.

Let it boil slowly and periodically give it a stir.

This is a bit of a waiting game because the sauce needs to thicken a bit so it doesn't just run all over your plate and will stick to the pasta, but without being too dry. The tomatoes will break down and express juice which you will need to boil off. This might take 30 minutes or more.

Taste it periodically, add more salt if you like and, if it tastes good, it is ready. Who cares if it is a little runny? You can leave it simmering while you cook the pasta.

Bring some water in a pot to the boil. Add the pasta and boil it until cooked (see Rules of Thumb for how to cook pasta).

When the pasta is cooked, drain and portion it out on a plate. Add as much sauce as you like then add loads of the grated cheese.

Perfetto!

Variations

There are plenty of options!

- Add cayenne when you fry the garlic.
- A teaspoon of crushed or whole fennel seeds adds a slight aniseed flavour – you will be surprised how seriously well this works.
- Traditional Spaghetti Bolognese uses both beef and pork mince. You can use only one type of mince if you like (beef, pork or chicken.) or any other combination.
- Add capsicum cut into small pieces along with the tomatoes.
- Add broccoli, broken into small florets, when you think the sauce has about 20 minutes of cooking to go.
- Add zucchini cut into small pieces and/or sliced mushrooms and/or frozen peas when you think the sauce has about 10 minutes to go (around about the time you are ready to start cooking the pasta).
- Add a decent slurp of brown beer or stout along with the tomatoes. Too much can make the sauce bitter. Add some sugar if you think it needs it.
- Add any fresh herbs that you may have (parsley, coriander, thyme, etc) when you think the sauce is ready for serving. If you only have dried herbs, add them with the tomatoes.

If you can get your hands on some parmesan cheese, it is simply superb grated and loaded on top of a plate of this recipe. DO NOT, under any circumstances, be tempted by dried parmesan!

Left-Overs

Reheat any pasta and sauce together in a pot with the lid on and at low heat to stop it sticking. You might have to add some water.

Cook more pasta if needed.

The sauce is also great on a roast spud or toast.

Roasted Chicken Pieces with Lemon and Tomatoes

This dish is remarkably simple and astoundingly good. Once you've made it and eaten the result, trust me, you won't stop cooking it.

The juices are wonderful soaked up with buttered bread.

Essential Ingredients

Garlic (the more the better)

Chicken pieces (enough to fill the bottom of a deep baking dish or tray, thighs are best but any will do)

Small tomatoes (cherry tomatoes)

Olive oil

Parsley

Lemon

Salt

Optional Ingredients

Cayenne pepper

Olives

Limes

Bacon

Other herbs

Directions

Heat your oven to 180C (350F).

Slice the garlic and spread the slices around the bottom of the baking dish or tray.

Cover the bottom of the baking dish or tray with the pieces of chicken, skin side up (it doesn't matter if you chicken is without the skin).

Scatter the cherry tomatoes around the tray and in the gaps between the chicken pieces if there are any. Prick or cut them all so the juice can come out when they are cooking.

Mix the following in a bowl: a good slurp of olive all, salt, the zest of the lemon and the parsley (chopped). Mix it all together with your hand and spread it over the chicken pieces.

Chuck it in the oven for about 45 minutes. Cut open a piece of chicken and if it isn't cooked through stick it back in the oven. Ideally the chicken will be browned on top but don't try too hard to achieve that as you might over-cook it and dry it out.

Good to go.

Variations

- Add cayenne pepper to the bowl of oil, salt, lemon zest and chopped parsley.
- Spread olives around at the same time as you do the tomatoes.
- Add lime zest instead of lemon zest.
- Add a bacon rasher (chopped small) to the bowl of oil, salt, lemon zest and chopped parsley.
- Replace the parsley or add with other herbs such as coriander or thyme.

Left-Overs

You can eat any left-overs cold from the fridge (the juices will have formed a lovely jelly).

You can also de-bone the cold chicken and cut it up for sandwiches.

If you put the left-over chicken in the fridge using the dish or tray you baked it in, use aluminium foil to cover it. You can then simply put it back in the oven to reheat it, with the aluminium cover in place to stop it from drying out.

Green Fish Part I

Sooner or later you will get hold of some fish, whether you have caught it yourself or someone has given it to you.

You can just fry it of course but I think this is a better idea.

It is called green fish because that's what I called it to get my son Hugo to eat it, and because it has a load of parsley in it. I also used to steam a load of mixed veg, mash them and squeeze the liquid out before adding to the recipe so he got the veg he wasn't keen on as well as the fish. But that is a variation rather than core recipe.

Don't be scared by the ingredients – this is easy.

Essential Ingredients

Fresh fish. Salmon is really good but it can be done with any fish as long as it doesn't have bones in it. DO NOT use defrosted fish as it will be sloppy.

Knob of fresh ginger

A lime

Egg

Corn flour

Parsley

Something spicy like wasabi paste, cayenne pepper, chopped fresh chilis, etc

Optional Ingredients

Any veg that you might like to steam and add as described above.

Lemon or other citrus to replace or add to the lime. Especially if you are using salmon, a citrus addition cuts through the fish oil and makes it less heavy. Ginger does the same thing.

You can use plain flour instead of corn flour, just not as good and you have to cook it enough that it doesn't taste floury.

Fresh coriander and/or mint to replace or add to the parsley. You can use dried herbs but they won't be as good and, in the case of coriander, won't be green.

Sesame or coconut oil are nice flavours for this type of Asian'ish dish, but it is expensive and you won't use it very often.

Directions

Make sure that the fish has no bones in it and the skin is off.

The easiest way to get rid of fish skin if you don't have a sharp knife is to put the fish on a plate, skin up, and pour a small amount of boiling water over it. The skin will curl up and it will be easy to take off by hand.

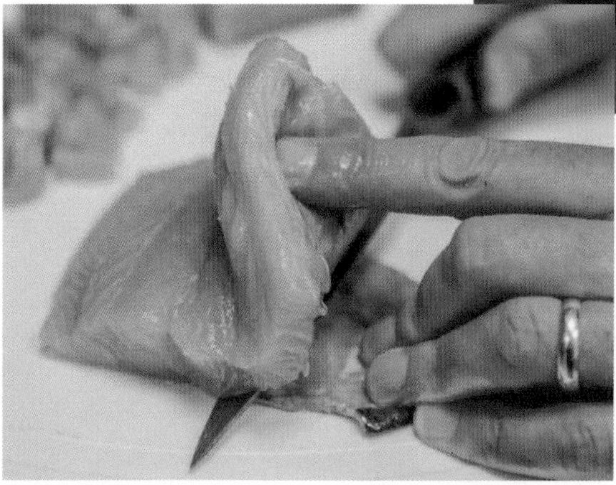

Cut the fish into pieces about the size of your finger-nail and put it in a bowl to mix with the other ingredients.

Peel the ginger and either cut it into very, very small pieces or grate it and add it to the bowl.

Grate the zest off the lime. If you can't grate it, use a knife to take the outer most layer of skin off and cut it up very, very small.

Chop up the parsley and/or other herbs and add them. The more the better really as this is meant to be aromatic!

Add the heat (wasabi paste, cayenne pepper or chopped fresh chilis).

Chuck in an egg and then mix it all up.

Gradually add enough flour so that the mix starts to become a little gloopy and the pieces stick a bit to each other

There is no alternative to experience in doing this. Better to add too little when you first do this because if it doesn't stick together when you cook it, it is no big deal.

Spoon the mix into heated oil in a frying pan and pat it down a bit so it flattens a little, let it cook and, when it is browned on one side, flip it and do the same on the other side.

That's it. Good to go.

Left-Overs

Cold from the fridge is great. Or just plonk one in a sandwich.

Green Fish Part II

I studied Chemical Engineering with a small (select? Yeh right!) cadre of about 30 students, which had a remarkably high proportion of women given the time. Almost universally, me and my male colleagues were doing the course because we liked blowing things up. I do not know why the women wanted to do the course but almost none of them still do engineering at the time of writing this cook-book.

My good friend Tanya went on to do an MBA at INSEAD and become a successful international banker, which gave her the opportunity to be feted by important people in numerous exotic countries and try their delights! Her email competitions with the heading of "guess what I just ate!" were keenly fought over and I still await my prize for correctly guessing "ducks' tongues".

Upon sighting an early draft of this cook-book, and inspired by Green Fish Part I, Tanya thought it was time to take it up a notch. Green in name is not the same as green in mouth! And we should be deprived no more....

Photographic Note: I suspect no-one is touching these foods without a forklift, PPE or sticks for a reason.

It's time for a brief intermission to savour the delight of food you do not need to prepare, but instead which requires simple tenacity, hard work and diligence to acquire. If you succeed, your mates at university will be in awe of you.

There are two "green fish" to watch for in the land of true gastronomes.

*The first is **Greenland shark**. Nature forgot any elegance when creating this lumpy blob with stunted pectoral fins that help it trawl through icy darkness in the Arctic.*

While their fat noses and gaping mouths give the shark a dull-witted appearance, they are actually not as dumb as they may appear. Greenland shark meat has evolved (or devolved) to a state that is extremely toxic when fresh due to high levels of urea and trimethylamine N-oxide. Having no use for eyes, the sharks also often live with worm-like parasites that dangle from their eyeballs in a form of watery ballet [Editor's note: I think the word "festoon" should be in here somewhere]. *They eat anything alive, fresh or rotten, and for anyone except an Icelandic fisherman, have made the distinction of netting them about as welcome as stepping in a bog of dog vomit. The message is clearly, "leave me alone".*

*Properly fermented, however, the Greenland shark is legendary, particularly in Iceland where its considered a delicacy (**Hákarl**).*

The Icelanders cure it with gusto in a highly sophisticated plastic bucket fermentation process, thereafter hanging it to dry for four to five months.

The result is an eagerly sought-after collection of soft lumps of goo with attractive mucous consistency, strong ammonia-rich smell reminiscent of toilet cleaner, and the prerequisite fishy taste.

If you are talented enough to acquire any, serve it on toothpicks, hold your nose and consume with anything of very high alcoholic percentage. According to Wikipedia, late chef Anthony Bourdain described fermented shark as "the single worst, most disgusting and terrible tasting thing" he had ever eaten. Still-swearing chef Gordon Ramsay challenged Top Gears' James May to a modern-day duel to eat fermented shark on The F Word. *Ramsay unfortunately spat it out, but May was able to get it down while graciously, perhaps not, recommending it highly.*

The second green fish candidate is called **Surströmming.** *In contrast to the Greenland shark, this is a cute little Baltic Sea herring traditional to Swedish cuisine since at least 500 years ago that does not look at all stupid.*

Lightly salted and eaten whole, it appears with a brackish green hue in the can and has the magical effect of turning human skin the same grey green, and/or emptying the contents of your stomach.

Either way, the little fish punches way above its weight and can be acquired online and shipped from Sweden at lightning speed, labelled as "camping supplies".

Neither of the above require any cooking preparation at all, and certainly warrant your very own beer night duels with close friends and potential romantic interests. Leftovers? Save for the parents to visit.

Schnitz

No intro is necessary – everyone knows what a chicken schnitzel is.

Essential Ingredients

Lots of oil

Fresh chicken breast

Eggs

Packet of bread crumbs

Lemon

Salt

Optional Ingredients

Cayenne pepper

Parsley

Cheese

Sliced ham

Directions

You will need three large plates.

Slice the chicken breasts with a sharp knife so that you get thin slices. If you cut them too thick (maybe you only have a blunt knife?), wrap each slice in cling film, lay it on your bench or any flat surface and bash it with a heavy pot, or anything else that is flat, until it is nice and thin. Put these on one plate.

Crack on egg onto another plate and whisk it a bit (use a fork if you don't have a whisk). It doesn't have to be perfectly whisked – you just want to break down the egg white a bit.

Put plenty of breadcrumbs onto the third plate. If you can't buy a packet of bread crumbs you can grate your own but it is tedious (although easier if you freeze the bread first). Grate some lemon zest onto the breadcrumbs and add some salt.

Heat plenty of oil in a frying pan.

Line up the plates with the frying pan like a conveyor belt – chicken slices, egg, breadcrumbs and pan.

Dip each slice into the egg so it gets a coating on each side and do the same with the bread crumbs before putting it into the pan.

Do this for each one.

You might need to add some more lemon zest and salt to the breadcrumbs for each slice so each has plenty of lemon and salt. Also keep an eye on the oil level in the pan as the breadcrumbs soak up loads of oil.

The schnitzel should have browned breadcrumbs stuck to the chicken. If you aren't sure whether they are ready just cut one open and check that the chicken is cooked through.

Done.

Variations

- Add cayenne pepper to the bread crumbs along with the lemon zest and salt to give it some heat.
- Add finely chopped parsley or any other herb to the breadcrumbs.
- Add sliced cheese to the top of your cooked schnitzel and melt it under the griller.
- Add thinly sliced ham to the top of your cooked schnitzel and then add cheese on top and melt it under the griller.
- Schnitzel Sandwich: Stick the schnitzel between two slices of buttered bread.

Left-Overs

You can reheat a schnitzel (just do it thoroughly!) but they are perfectly good cold either by themselves or in a sandwich.

Pumpkin Soup—the Ultimate Guide (with added pumpkin lifehack)

This recipe comes from my wonderful friend Emma Macdonald, who learned everything about food from her mum Valerie Macdonald!

Along with our respective spouses, Clare and Chimpy, we shared one of the all-time great lunches at Bistrot Laguna Blu, on Lago Maggiore at Reno Di Leggiuno. Lago Maggiore is spectacular, with vistas overlooking the lake and the mountains behind. When we arrived, our friend and Restaurant Manager, Monica, warned us that a large table in the restaurant was occupied by a group from Milan, which had bused up for the day and might get rowdy. "No worries", we weren't so quiet ourselves once we had a few vini under our belts. We went on to have a fantastic lunch with wonderful food and drinks and lots of laughs as usual.

The group did indeed make some noise. They were a professional opera troop and fully prepared to entertain the restaurant for a bit with a few improvised pieces, including Nessun Dorma and 'O Sole Mio, while walking around the tables. It was mesmerizing stuff!

Anyway, this recipe is Emma's, is subject to copyright and so has been reproduced here with a minimum of editing and addition of some possible variations at the end.

The first time I made this, I used cayenne pepper, garam masala, curry powder and turmeric (because pumpkins simply aren't orange enough for me!) I also used a potato masher instead of a stick blender, to see if the soup would work for students who might not have such a beast. I'm here to tell you it works a treat. I would suggest however that you cut the onions finely and cook them slowly to make them as soft as possible. Or just get a blender. I also forgot to buy the coriander, yoghurt and chilis. It was still fabulous!

It is a simply wonderful soup and you won't regret making it and playing around with it.

So what is the little pumpkin life hack?

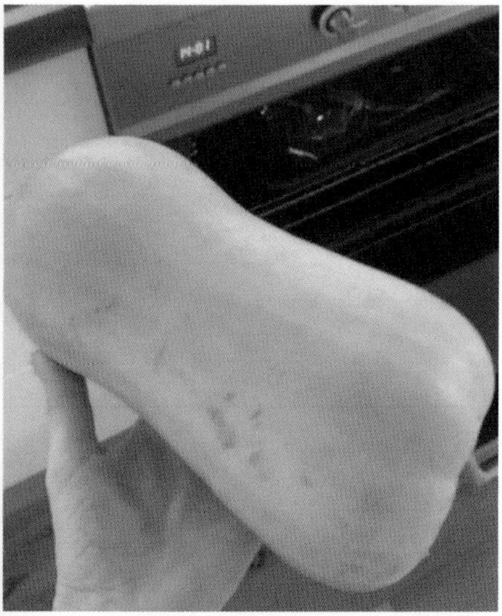

It is....(drumroll please) that you can cook your Butternut pumpkin by throwing it in a 180C oven for one and a half hours. Don't cut it—don't even wash it. Just put it on a tray (to catch the drips) and let it roast all on its own.

Once it has cooled, you can peel the skin back and scoop out the seeds, leaving nothing but sweet, moist pumpkin pulp—great to use in soups, or mash as a side, or use as toddler and baby food. You will never look at a pumpkin the same way again, we swear—and think of all those knife injuries we have saved you from because, there's no denying, cutting pumpkin is a bitch of a job.

But back to the soup.

Ingredients

1 Butternut pumpkin whole-roasted

1 can coconut cream (or milk if you prefer)

2 white onions chopped

Some spices, including cumin, coriander, garam masala or ginger

Half to one cup of stock

The rind and juice of an orange

A bunch of chopped fresh coriander

Greek yoghurt to dollop in at the end

1 red chilli finely sliced as garnish

Directions

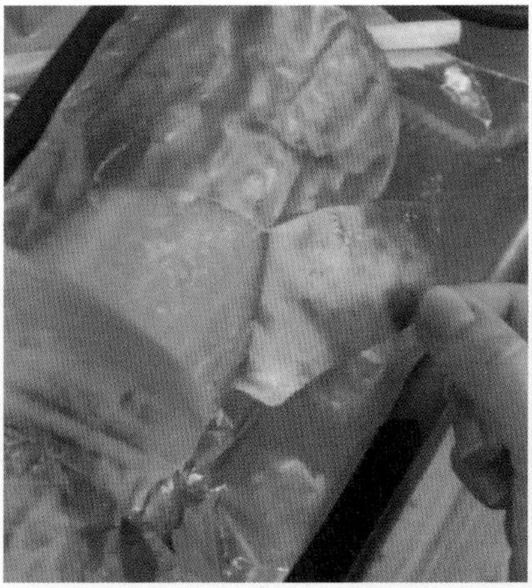

Chuck your pumpkin in the oven in the early afternoon and cook it, then let it cool.

Later that afternoon, fry up your onion in some olive oil in a large casserole pot.

Throw in some spices—whatever you like and whatever you have to hand. Cook it all for just a few minutes.

Peel your pumpkin and scoop out the flesh and then add it to your cooked onion.

Add some stock and then pour in your coconut cream. Grate in your orange rind and squeeze in the juice of your orange.

When it has cooled sufficiently, stick in your stick blender and blend it until smooth.

Add your coriander assuming you aren't a coriander-hater. Serve in a bowl with a dollop of yoghurt and sprinkle some red chilli over.

If you want to make a meal of it, whip up some garlic bread, or grill some sourdough with garlic, butter and parmesan. It almost makes a cold snap worth it.

Variations

Pumpkin soup is remarkably flexible. Here are some suggestions.

- Replace the pumpkin with sweet potato. Or use the pumpkin and add sweet potato and/or potatoes.
- Peel and slice some ginger and throw it in before the blending. You will have to fish out the ginger when you are eating it but it will have given the soup a wonderful flavour.
- Use a mandarin instead of an orange.

The coconut milk in this recipe gives it a real Asian or Sub-Continental feel. You can add the following ingredients too, but it will work better by replacing the coconut milk with more stock.

- Bacon cut into small pieces and added with the onions.
- Carraway seeds. This is a rarely used spice but aren't hard to get. Just add it when you add the other spices.

Left-Overs

Just reheat.

Roast Chook

Chicken is the cheapest meat you will be able to get your hands on so use it a lot!

A good old roast is always a winner and dead simple. You will need one or two roasting trays and an oven big enough to put them in.

Essential Ingredients

Whole Chicken

Oil

Salt

Gravy mix

Optional Ingredients

Cayenne pepper

Root vegetables for roasting: potatoes, carrots, pumpkin, sweet potatoes, beetroot, swede, turnips, etc

Other vegetables for roasting: capsicums, zucchini, mushrooms.

Vegetables for steaming or boiling: peas, broccoli, cauliflower.

Cayenne pepper

Take a look at the Variations section of this recipe – there are so many things you can do that the ingredients can't be listed here.

Directions

Put the chicken in the roasting tray, drizzle some oil over it and wipe it with your hands thoroughly over the chicken and then sprinkle with salt.

The chicken will take about 45 minutes to cook in the oven (at 180C). After that time it will need checking for two things.

1. Is it cooked through? Slice open the thigh (the meat between the drumstick and the body of the chicken) and if the juice that flows out is clear then it is done.
2. Is the skin crispy? If not, turn the oven up high and leave it in for a little longer until it is golden brown.

When the chicken is cooked or near to cooked, make some gravy following the instructions on the pack (or later in this recipe). Remember, you can never have enough gravy because any excess can be mopped up on buttered bread.

To serve it, just cut the bits off the chicken you want to eat. Most people have a favourite part. Let anyone you are eating with go for the breast and drumsticks and keep the thighs for yourself – they have more fat on them and are therefore tastier and juicier. Being on the bone also provides more flavour.

Pour loads of gravy over the chicken and anything else you have cooked with it.

Variations

- Add cayenne pepper when you sprinkle salt on the chicken.
- Slice up some garlic into thin slithers. With a small knife, make some insertions into the fleshy parts of the chicken and insert a slither into each. The garlic will permeate the meat.
- Mash together a fair amount of butter, crushed garlic and some finely chopped rosemary, or any other herb for that matter. A fork is good for the mashing. Gently insert the mash under the skin on the breast of the chicken. This is actually a relatively delicate job because you don't want to rip the skin. You might need a small pair of scissors to cut any membranes joining the skin to the flesh of the breasts. The butter will melt and transfer the garlic and rosemary flavours around the chicken.
- Make roasted root vegetables. Cut the vegetables into the size you want them but remember that the harder vegetables, like beetroot and carrots, take longer to cook than the soft ones, like pumpkin. Par-boil them together, which means put them in a pot of water and boil them until the outsides are soft but they are still somewhat firm on the inside. Drain them, return to the pot, drizzle a load of oil and some salt (and cayenne pepper) and then mix them roughly with a large spoon or shake the pot so that the vegetables start to break up a little bit. The broken bits will brown really nicely. They go in the oven at the same time as the chicken. Check them when you check the chicken. If some of them are too hard, cut them in half and put them back in the oven.
- Boiling or steaming peas, broccoli, cauliflower, etc is easy. Again, remember than the harder ones will cook quicker than the softer ones. They will only take 10 minutes or so once the water has boiled so cook them last. If they are cooked too early for the chicken and other vegetables, just remove the water, return them to the hot pan and put the lid on. This will stop them going cold or over-cooking.

Make other roasted vegetables. You can also roast vegetables like capsicums, zucchini, mushrooms, etc but they will take less time than the root vegetables if you are making them.

Just slice them thickly, coat them in oil and salt and add to the other vegetables about 20 minutes after you have put the root vegetables in the oven.

Real gravy 3 ways:

- Pan gravy is made by removing the chicken and any vegetables from the pan, sprinkling plain flour into the pan (a tablespoon or two) and stirring it into any juices in the pan, adding hot water slowly while you heat the pan on the stove. If you add the water before the flour you have lumps everywhere. When it is boiling and thickened a bit it is ready. To be honest, I find this a bit of a trial and in the meantime the chicken is cooling. So….
- If you have a baking pan that has a rack that fits into the bottom and will keep the chicken off the bottom of the pan, add water to the pan before putting the chicken on the grill into the pan. Make sure the water level is below the grill though, you don't want the bottom of the chicken in the water. Cook the chicken in the oven as you normally would, remove it from the pan and put aside the water, which has caught all of the fat and juices that have come out of the chicken. Use this water (you might need to skim off the fat if there is too much) with packet gravy to make your gravy. It will have loads more flavour.
- Just make packet gravy for everyone and, while no-one is looking, scrape all of the tacky juices out of the pan and eat it all yourself, straight with a

spoon or with buttered bread. This stuff is so incredibly rich and like chicken flavour on steroids. Addictive!

Left-Overs

So many possibilities!

- Pick the Carcass. My son Hugo and I would bring the cold chicken and vegetable out of the fridge, put it in the middle of the table and rip it apart with our hands. Great fun.
- Roast chicken and vegetable sandwiches. Mash up some avocado if you have it (use butter if you don't) and load up a monster sandwich with cut up chicken and sliced left over vegetables.
- You can add the chopped up leftovers to almost any of the non-fish recipes in this book, especially Paupers' Pizza, Frittata, Roast Potatoes, Lager-Frenzy Fry Up and Downright Slow Pasta.

Fried Gnocchi

This is a dead simple variation on regulation gnocchi and is amazingly good and super cheap!

The best gnocchi I ever had was at Bistro Laguna Blu, at Reno Di Leggiuno on Lago Maggiore.

Clare and I were at the bar drinking more than most Italians would normally be happy about, especially without eating, and we were pretty merry. Giuliano, our friend and the manager, kept asking us if we wanted to eat anything but we said no, we weren't hungry. In the end, he just put a plate of gnocchi in a creamy gorgonzola sauce in front of us and we ate the lot. Simply superb.

But for quick and easy this recipe is a winner. The gnocchi will be a little chewy and with a golden crust, chockers with the flavour of the other ingredients.

Essential Ingredients

Packet of fresh gnocchi

Oil

Lemon

Garlic

Cayenne pepper

Salt

Optional Ingredients

You can add just about anything to this as long as it is cut small and won't generate a sauce – the gnocchi has to fry. But don't add much because this recipe is about the gnocchi.

Yes you can add cheese but I think it is better without.

Directions

Boil the gnocchi according to the instructions. Drain them. At this point they are cooked but you still want to fry them.

Slice the garlic and zest the lemon while the gnocchi is cooking.

Heat quite a bit of oil in a frying pan and add the gnocchi, moving them around quite a bit to stop them sticking together. When they are moving freely just let them fry for a while. What you want is for them to be golden brown on both sides. You might need to top up the oil as they will soak up quite a bit.

When the gnocchi are cooked on one side, add the other ingredients and turn the gnocchi to fry the other side.

This is about the only recipe I do where the garlic doesn't go into the pan before just about everything else. Reason is, learned through trial and error, the gnocchi takes a while to fry and if added at the start the garlic will over-cook, go brown (hopefully not black!) and be very bitter.

It will be ready when golden-brown on both sides but don't be afraid to take it out earlier if the other ingredients might over-cook. Simply spoon it out onto a plate.

Variations

You can also make this with any pasta. Just cook the pasta and drain it. Cook the sauce in a frying pan and add the pasta. You aren't trying to brown the pasta though, just make sure that it is heated through and has a nice coating of the sauce.

Left-Overs

You can reheat this dish but I usually just eat them cold straight from the fridge.

They are great reheated as part of a Lager-Frenzy Fry-Up!

Stir-Fry

There are thousands of stir fry recipes which show how versatile this dish is, so there is no excuse for ever getting bored with it. So I will show you how to make the last stir fry that I made myself, so you get the technique, and then provide some indication of how you can vary the recipe as you wish.

First a few things to know about stir frying.

- Stir frying uses loads of vegetables which are cooked very quickly and should have some crunch when served. So only use very fresh ingredients.
- Stir frying is fast so have each ingredient ready to go (ie peeled, cut up, etc) before you start cooking.
- In the section on Rules of Thumb at the start of this book, I mentioned that if you are cooking multiple vegetables together, you should cut them to a size that attempts to have them ready all at the same time. Stir frying is different and simpler. Just cut everything into a relatively small, similar size that will cook quickly. The ingredients are then added in turn, starting with the ones that will take longest to cook and gradually adding the rest that would take less time to cook. Each ingredient or group of ingredients should be cooked for only a minute or two before adding the next.
- It's a stir fry, so stir it perpetually. This helps the ingredients cook through at the same rate and hopefully stop water being expressed.
- Real stir fry is made in a wok or large, heavy pan, with lots of oil, under very high temperature. The objective is to flash fry the ingredients so that they seal, trapping in the goodness and flavour and preventing them from expressing liquid as they cook. You might well find that you only have a light pan or pot, which can lead to burning the ingredients, causing them to stick and potentially blackening the inside of you pot or pan. If that is the case just turn the temperature down. It will still be fine, even if the ingredients start to stew somewhat in its own liquid.

- This is the only recipe in this book where olive oil probably isn't the ideal oil to use. At higher temperatures the oil can start to smoke (effectively burning it) which will affect the flavour. If you have olive oil, try how high you can get the oil before it starts to smoke and then turn the temperature down if you have to. Alternatively, you can use another oil like sunflower oil, safflower oil or, my favourite because of the extra flavour it gives, sesame oil.
- You can easily serve this with rice to bulk it out. Because the stir fry cooks so quickly it is best to cook the rice first, drain it and then either put it back in the pot with a lid to make sure it doesn't get cold, or put it under hot water under the tap or water boiled in a kettle to reheat it.

Essential Ingredients (for my last stir fry)

Boneless chicken pieces

Soy sauce and teriyaki sauce. These keep almost indefinitely so a bottle of each will go a long way.

Lots of Garlic

Oil Onion

Carrots

Cayenne pepper

Capsicum

Baby corn

Broccoli

Zucchini

Baby spinach

Optional Ingredients

Almost any other meat, such as beef, pork, lamb, prawns, etc.

Any other Asian sauces, like fish sauce and oyster sauce.

Fresh chilis.

Any spices that you might like to add, like ground coriander, fennel seeds, etc.

Any vegetables that taste good when uncooked. I would steer clear of potatoes, pumpkin, beetroot, etc.

Unsalted cashews or any other peeled and unsalted nuts.

Directions

Slice the chicken fillets thinly, put them in a bowl and add some soy sauce and teriyaki sauce in equal measure. Let it marinade for at least half an hour if you have the time. The longer it marinades the better and overnight in the fridge is perfect, but not essential.

Thinly slice, chop or crush the garlic and add it to the marinating chicken.

When you are ready to cook, prepare the other ingredients.

Peel the carrot and cut it into matchsticks, about half as long as your index finger. Slice the onions and put them in a bowl with the carrot. Add the cayenne pepper to the bowl.

De-seed the capsicum and cut it into matchsticks, about the same size as the carrot. Do the same with the baby corn and put them in a separate bowl with the capsicum.

Cut the broccoli into small florets and slice thinly any broccoli stalk you may be using. Cut the zucchini into matchsticks, about the same size as your other matchsticks.

Wash the baby spinach and have it ready to go too. The baby spinach will wilt to almost nothing in the stir fry so don't be scared to use a lot!

When you are ready to cook, heat the oil at high temperature in your wok or pan.

Drain the chicken but reserve any marinade.

When the oil is hot, add the bowl of onions, carrots and cayenne pepper and stir fry for a couple of minutes.

Then add the bowl of chicken and garlic and stir fry until the chicken is no longer looking raw on the outside.

Then add the bowl of capsicum and baby corn and stir fry for a minute or two.

Then add the bowl of broccoli and zucchini and stir fry for a minute or two.

Then add the baby spinach and reserved marinade and stir fry until the spinach has wilted down.

Serve straight away.

Variations

- You don't have to use meat in this recipe. Try going vegetarian – it is still very good.
- Try different meats or even combinations of meats.
- Try the other Asian sauces either alone or in combination. All of these sauces tend to be salty so don't automatically reach for the salt if you decide not to use soy sauce.

- Since you are cutting up a load of vegetables anyway, why not try replacing the cayenne pepper with fresh chilis?
- Add any other spices that you might like to try. Best to put it in the wok or pan with the onions to bring out the flavour.
- Mix and match the vegetables depending on what you have or what is fresh wherever you shop.
- Add some crunch with the unsalted cashews or other nuts.

Left-Overs

You can re-heat this recipe or just eat cold, straight from the fridge.

Dips (WTF?)

There are a couple of really good reasons for making the dips in this book.

Firstly, they are fast, easy and great for having with any raw vegetables, bread, biscuits and sliced cheese you have lying around. You can use any sliced, raw vegetables that you don't need to cook to be edible, such as capsicum, zucchini, cucumber, carrots, celery, tomatoes, cabbage, radishes, etc, etc.

Secondly, if you think of them more as a sauce, you can have them with a load of other stuff, like on the Roast (or Baked) Potatoes or on toast with the Lager-Frenzy Fry Up earlier in this book.

As an example of how easy and great they can be, courtesy of Clare, try mixing curry powder into plain yoghurt, in increasing amounts until you get the taste you want. It doesn't get easier than that.

Garlic & Anchovy Dip

Turn your nose up at this all you like but I guarantee that once you have made this you will make it again! It is strong and pungent and not for the faint hearted, something like the Italian version of Vegemite, and we all know how addictive that stuff is.

Anchovies are a wonderful ingredient. The first time you taste them you will just think that they are over-salted, very strong fish. Which of course they are. But very quickly it will be "one for the pan, one for me".

This is great as a snack or as a main course, depending on what and how much you have to dip into it. If you have a bunch of left over fresh vegetables or just some bread, this works a treat. In fact, this works with stale bread too!

Essential Ingredients

Oil (preferably a good one like extra virgin olive oil – the oil is one of the features in this dip rather than just something to fry other stuff in)

Butter

Garlic

Anchovy fillets (no need for salt)

Optional Ingredients

Any sliced raw vegetables

Bread

Cayenne pepper

Pepper

Directions

Heat a load of butter and oil in a pan. When it melts, add the chopped or finely sliced garlic and some anchovy fillets and let them simmer slowly until the garlic is turning golden (not brown) and the anchovies have disintegrated and dissolved into the oil and butter.

Seriously, that is it. You have to serve it hot (or warm) because the butter will solidify as it cools. Just stick it in the middle of the table with whatever you have cut up or shredded for dipping into it.

Variations

- Add cayenne pepper when you heat the oil and butter to give it some zing.
- Add a load of pepper (cracked if you've got it,)

Left-Overs

Any left over dip can be kept covered in the fridge for ages as the oil and butter will preserve it. But when you take it out it will be semi-solid again so you will have to reheat it.

So many options! This stuff also works as a wonderful spread for other meals so try it on any meat (like the roast chicken recipe in this book) or sausages. It is also a wonderful lifter for a store-bought meat pie. It is also great when tossed onto pasta. I suspect might also be useful for a post-game rub-down.

Guac

During high-school I used to work in a fruit shop for pocket-money. Sunday lunch was always fish and chips with a coke in the lunchroom.

But Ernie, the owner, would take a slice of bread, cut up an avocado and eat it straight with salt.

He also had on the lunchroom shelves these large plastic jars full of oil and white amorphous blobs that I now know were home-made feta cheese.

At the time I turned my nose up at the thought of all that, but now, I would have the avocado and feta any day.

It is not possible to sing the praises of guacamole too much. But the big proviso is that you have a ripe avocado. Under-ripe avocadoes are hard and taste soapy – not good! And whatever you do, don't cook avocado. It is disgraceful.

Essential Ingredients

Ripe avocado(es)

Lemon

Salt

Optional Ingredients

Lime

Cayenne pepper

Fresh herbs, especially coriander

Tomato

Red onion (or any other kind of sweet onion)

Directions

There is a bit of a knack to getting the avocado flesh out of the fruit and free of the large seed in the middle. But it isn't hard. This is what I do.

- Holding the avocado in your hand, push a knife blade (not the pointy end) into the top of the fruit until you feel the resistance of the seed inside. With the knife still in the fruit, run the blade around the fruit, from the starting point at the top, through to the bottom and back up the other side to the top, all the while having the blade touching the seed. You can easily circumnavigate the avocado this way. Remove the knife.
- Twist the two halves of avocado so that they come apart with one half in each hand. On half will contain the seed, half exposed.
- Chop your knife blade (not the pointy end) onto the seed so that the blade penetrates the seed, but not too far. With the knife in the seed, twist the blade gently and the seed will free up from the flesh.
- Spoon the flesh from the skin of the fruit and onto a chopping board or plate.

Now use a fork to mash the avocado fruit. This should be very easy if the fruit is ripe.

Mix in some lemon juice and salt, adding more if needed.

Strictly speaking, the lemon juice isn't an essential ingredient because salted avocado is great by itself. However, in addition to tasting great, the acid in the juice will stop the mashed avocado from oxidising and going brown, which it does pretty quickly. Oxidised avocado still tastes great but it doesn't look too hot.

Variations

- Try lime juice instead of lemon juice.
- Add any of the optional ingredients at the same time as the lemon and salt. This is a recipe where everything just gets chucked in together.
- If you want to add some tomato, it is best to first de-seed the tomato and cut it up finely. This stops all of the tomato juice turning the guac into a runny mess.
- If you want to add onion, cut it up very finely.

Whatever you add, remember that the avocado is the main ingredient so don't add too much of anything else.

Left-Overs

Guac keeps in the fridge so take out any left overs and eat it however you like, including just spooning it in.

Tzatz

It is easy to just buy tzatziki in almost any supermarket, but home-made is much better and it is easy to make. Strictly speaking, tzatz should be made with Greek yoghurt, which is thicker than normal yoghurt. But regulation, plain yoghurt works fine.

Essential Ingredients

Plain yoghurt

Cucumber

Lemon

Oil

Mint

Garlic (crushed or finely chopped)

Salt

Optional Ingredients

Other fresh herbs, such as dill or coriander

Cayenne pepper

Lime

Directions

First you need to deseed your cucumber. Doing this removes a lot of the liquid from the cucumber and makes sure you don't end up with a runny mess.

To do this, cut the cucumber in half length-ways, exposing the seeds in the centre. Then use a teaspoon to scoop the seeds out of the cucumber.

Then cut the cucumber into very small pieces.

The cucumber pieces then simply get added along with the other ingredients to the yoghurt and mixed together. Don't add too much lemon juice, salt and garlic. It is best to add a bit, taste it and add some more if you think it needs it.

Variations

Try lime juice instead of lemon juice.

Left-Overs

Tzatz keeps in the fridge so take out any left overs and eat it however you like.

Salads - The Not So Sexy Stuff

I can't say that I'm a great salad fan. Typically, they are a bit of a side show to the main event, unless they are more complex and use more ingredients than what this book is about.

There may nonetheless be a couple of reasons why you might want to make a salad.

- You are asked to bring one to a BBQ.
- You offer to bring one to the BBQ because bringing meat or another dish is too expensive.
- You want to impress someone with a side to one of the other recipes in this book.

Fair enough – here are a couple of simple but very good salads.

Middle East Salad

You really couldn't come across a simpler and cheaper salad than this. And it is actually pretty good.

Essential Ingredients

Roughly equal quantities of:

- Tomatoes
- Cucumbers
- Red onions

Oil

Lemon

Salt

Optional Ingredients

Any salady stuff that you can cut into small pieces, like capsicum, broccoli, etc.

Lime or other citrus or vinegar to replace the lemon.

Garlic

Cayenne pepper

Sumac (you probably won't have heard of this mild spice but it is great with this salad).

Herbs, like parsley, mint and/or coriander.

Directions

Cut the tomatoes into about four pieces each, scoop out and discard the seeds and juice.

Cut the cucumbers length ways and using a tea-spoon scrape out and discard all of the seeds.

The reason for doing this is that the seeds and juice will make the salad too runny and left overs won't last as long with everything soggy.

Peel the red onions.

Cut the tomatoes, cucumbers and onions into very small pieces and put them into a large bowl.

Add a fair amount of olive oil, juice of half a lemon and salt. Mix it all up.

Taste it and add more lemon juice and salt if you want to.

Best to put the salad in the fridge before you serve it – salads are typically nicest and fresher tasting when cold.

Variations

- You can add other salad ingredients that can be cut into small pieces but remember, this is meant to be simple and easy and cheap.
- The lemon is there to cut through the oil and add flavour. This recipe needs some acid! But you can replace the lemon with any other citrus or vinegar. If using vinegar, add it a little at a time and taste before adding more.
- Very finely cut or crushed garlic adds loads of flavour, but don't overdo it.
- Cayenne pepper will spice it up. If you can get sumac then it works perfectly with this salad and you can be heavy handed with it.
- Herbs also work really well, especially aromatic herbs like mint and coriander.

Left-Overs

This salad will keep for a few days in the fridge so just take it out and tuck in.

Potato Salad

This salad will kill you.

Essential Ingredients

Potatoes (use enough to feed the number of people who will be eating it)

Sour cream

Bacon

Mustard (a few teaspoons)

Vinegar

Optional Ingredients

Fresh herbs, especially chives and parsley

Onion

Garlic

Cayenne pepper

Directions

Cut the potatoes into bite-size pieces (not too small) and boil them until they are tender but hold some firmness. You don't want the potatoes to fall apart while making this salad.

Chop up the bacon into small pieces and fry it until you are happy with it. Then add all of the other ingredients into the pan except the vinegar. DO NOT throw away the bacon fat before you do this!

Add a small splash of vinegar, taste it and add some more until you are happy with it. It should be slightly acidic but you don't want the vinegar to overpower the other flavours.

Add some pepper. Salt probably won't be needed because of the bacon, but taste it and add salt if you want.

Drain the potatoes and add them to the pan while they are still hot.

Serve it up.

Variations

- If you want to include chopped onion and/or sliced garlic, add them to the pan at the same time as the bacon. Fry them until they are soft and golden.
- If you want to add cayenne pepper, also add it to the pan with the bacon.
- You can use any type of vinegar so feel free to experiment.
- You can also use any type of mustard. Seeded mustard provides a nice texture.

Left-Overs

This salad is tastiest when served warm but it will keep for a few days in the fridge and can be served cold.

About the Author

Striped sometimes cooks.

Notes

Printed in Great Britain
by Amazon

12960525R00058